I Am Somebody Special

Author:

Dr. Rebecca Dashiell-Mitchell

Illustrator:

John A. Floyd, Jr.

To order additional copies of this book, contact:
Xlibris
844-714-8691
www.Xlibris.com
Orders@Xlibris.com

ISBN: Softcover   979-8-3694-1665-5
        EBook   979-8-3694-1663-1

Print information available on the last page

Rev. date: 02/19/2024

From Granberri to... Isaac Anthony,
Alexander Justin and Olivia Jasmine!

Introduction

As of May 2013, this poem of affirmation has been dedicated to each Horizons Atlanta Clark Atlanta University Young Scholar. During morning gatherings, mid-day, and in closing Excel-ebrations our Young Scholars enthusiastically participate in the "call response" recitation of "I Am Somebody Special!" These are the moments when we discuss and embrace personal experiences of gratitude, empathy, grit, and determination. Our "call response" recitation creates and confirms one's personal image as a 21st century scholar.

Today I dedicate this poem of affirmation to the Young Scholars of Horizons Atlanta and Horizons National as a springboard for discussing friendships, trusting relationships, purpose, and a sense of belonging. Our children are society's passport to the future. I salute each teacher, each parent, each grandparent, and each community partner who share my *"Let's Do Something"* vision of supporting 21st century heroes and she-roes!

For the young, self-concept is derived from the amalgamation of experiences encountered and absorbed from the moment of birth until the fullness of current age. Self-concept is the personal image that we create and hold of ourselves due to the level of learning and the intensity of emotional-social- psychological interactions that beckons opportunity for new change and greater growth.

Through this poem of affirmation, "I am Somebody Special," children proudly voice how they see themselves through the lens of self-love, self-esteem, self-efficacy, and self-reliance!

I Am Somebody Special.
I Can Think and Solve Challenges!

I Take Care of Myself!

I Also Help Others!

I Am Somebody Special!

I Am Somebody Special.
I Like to Run, Jump, and Have Fun!

I Am Somebody Special!
I Belong to a Family. I Get Along
With My Family and My Friends!

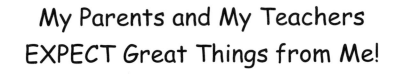

My Parents and My Teachers
EXPECT Great Things from Me!

I Am Somebody UNIQUELY Special.

I Am Somebody Special!
Did You Know? Did You Know?
I Am A Scholar!

YES, I Am Somebody Special!

I Am Somebody Special!

My NAME is _____ .

I weigh _____ pounds.

I am _____ feet and _____ inches tall.

_____

MY PHOTOGRAPH

_____

I have read _____ books this summer!

I speak many languages: _____ , _____ ,

_____ , and _____ .

My BIRTHDAY is ... _____

Today's Date: _____ .

I Can Think and Solve Challenges!

For example, One day I...

_____

_____

_____

_____

_____

_____

_____

_____

_____

_____

_____

I Take Care of Myself!

Would you believe I take care of myself by ...

_____

_____

_____

_____

_____

_____

_____

_____

_____

_____

_____

_____

_____

I Also Help Others!

I really, really enjoy helping others when I ...

_____

_____

_____

_____

_____

_____

_____

_____

_____

_____

_____

_____

_____

_____

I like to do many things!

You may call the things I like to do, "hobbies."

Accordingly, I like to...

_____

_____

_____

_____

_____

_____

_____

_____

_____

_____

_____

_____

_____

I Belong To A Family!

Let me tell you about my family and my friends!

My Family ...

_____

_____

_____

_____

_____

My Friends' Names Are...

_____

_____

_____

_____

_____

I believe my friends are special too!

My Parents and My Teachers EXPECT Great Things from Me!

Let me tell YOU what my PARENTS EXPECT from me!

- _____
- _____
- _____
- _____
- _____
- _____
- _____

Let me tell YOU what my TEACHERS EXPECT from me!

- _____
- _____
- _____
- _____
- _____
- _____
- _____

I Am Somebody Uniquely Special! Did You Know?

Right NOW, I like to...

○ _____

○ _____

○ _____

○ _____

○ _____

○ _____

○ _____

In my future I will...

○ _____

○ _____

○ _____

○ _____

○ _____

○ _____

○ _____

Did YOU Know, I Am A Scholar?

I am so thankful for the wonderful people in my family, my school, and in my community, who encourage and inspire me to achieve my dreams. I call these wonderful people my Heroes and my She-roes!

I am a Young Scholar and I am so proud to tell you about one of my favorite Heroes and one of my favorite She-roes.

My SHE-ROE: Ms./Mrs./Dr. _____

                      First Name   **Last Name**

_____

_____

_____

_____

My HEROE: Mr./Dr. _____

                      First Name   **Last Name**

_____

_____

_____

_____

Yes, Did You Know? I Am A Scholar!

I Am Somebody Special!

I Am Somebody Special!
I Can Think and Solve Challenges!
I Take Care of Myself!
I Also Help Others!

I Am Somebody Special!
I like to Run, Jump and Have Fun!
I Am Somebody Special!

I Belong to A Family!
I Get Along with My Family and My Friends!
My Parents and Teachers Expect Great
Things From Me!

I Am Somebody Uniquely Special!
Did you Know? Did you Know?
I Am A Scholar!

AUTHOR: Rebecca Dashiell-Mitchell, Ed.D. May 29, 2013

About the Author -
Dr. Rebecca Dashiell-Mitchell

Step into the enchanting world of Dr. Rebecca Dashiell-Mitchell, a spirited native of Boston, Massachusetts, whose heart beats with the rhythm of education and the magic of storytelling. For over four decades, Dr. Dashiell-Mitchell has been a guiding light for children and families, from the culturally rich streets of her birth town to the vibrant city of Atlanta.

In her captivating journey as a Curriculum and Instruction Assistant Professor at Clark Atlanta University, she not only inspires the "critical eye, critical ear, and critical heart" of future teachers, she ventures into the realm of children's literature and digital storytelling. However, the true sparkle in her storytelling crown lies the fact that Dr. Dashiell-Mitchell is an educator; a published poet, "BECCA DASH," and Director of the Horizons Atlanta Clark Atlanta University Program. As one who loves teaching, learning, and exploring, she believes that words have the power to build bridges across cultures and generations. As a wife, mother, and Granberri she is most determined to make certain that children are empowered to become the hero/she-roe of their own story!

About the Illustrator –
Mr. John A. Floyd, Jr.

Mr. John A. Floyd, Jr. was born in Fort Bragg, North Carolina and has traveled extensively as a child of military parents. His natural drawing ability was immediately noticed in kindergarten. From an early age and through-out his schooling several awards, medals, ribbons, and plaques were bestowed. Mr. Floyd was influenced by several master artists of diverse artistic mediums. Today, Mr. John A. Floyd., Jr., a renowned illustrator, specializes in portraits, sculptures, signs, and murals.

Printed in the United States
by Baker & Taylor Publisher Services